JUV/E8
FIC
PACKARD

EASTSI

Chicago Public Lit

W9-BBP-820
Where is Jake?

Where Is Jake?

DISCARD

Chicago Public Library
Vodak/East Side Branch
3710 E. 106th St.
Chicago, IL 60617

Where Is Jake?

Written by Mary Packard

Illustrated by Joy Allen

My First READER

children's press®

A Division of Scholastic Inc.
New York   Toronto   London   Auckland   Sydney
Mexico City   New Delhi   Hong Kong
Danbury, Connecticut

Library of Congress Cataloging-in-Publication Data

Packard, Mary.
  Where is Jake? / written by Mary Packard ; illustrated by Joy Allen.–
1st ed.
      p. cm. – (My first reader)
Summary: Illustrations and easy-to-read text show how, as two children
search for their dog Jake, he stays just a step ahead of them.
  ISBN 0-516-22957-5 (lib. bdg.)   0-516-24641-0 (pbk.)
  [1. Dogs–Fiction. 2. Lost and found possessions–Fiction.] I. Allen,
Joy, ill. II. Title. III. Series.
  PZ7.P1247Wh 2003
  [E]–dc21

                        2003003699

Text © 1990 Nancy Hall, Inc.
Illustrations © 2003 Joy Allen
Published in 2003 by Children's Press
A Division of Scholastic Inc.
All rights reserved. Published simultaneously in Canada.
Printed in the United States of America.

CHILDREN'S PRESS and associated logos are trademarks and or registered trademarks of
Scholastic Library Publishing. SCHOLASTIC and associated logos are trademarks and or
registered trademarks of Scholastic Inc.

  2 3 4 5 6 7 8 9 10 R 12 11 10 09 08 07 06 05 04

EAS

R0404735017

Note to Parents and Teachers

Once a reader can recognize and identify the 16 words
used to tell this story, he or she will be able to read successfully
the entire book. These 16 words are repeated throughout the story,
so that young readers will be able to easily recognize
the words and understand their meaning.

The 16 words used in this book are:

above	Jake
down	out
eat	there
he	time
hi	to
hiding	under
in	up
is	where

Chicago Public Library
Vodak/East Side Branch
3710 E. 106th St.
Chicago, IL 60617

Where is Jake?

JAKE

Is he hiding?

Is he in?

Is he out?

Is he under?

Is he above?

Is he up?

Is he down?

Jake?

23

Where is Jake?

Time to eat!

Hi there, Jake!

ABOUT THE AUTHOR

Mary Packard has been writing children's books for as long as she can remember. Packard lives in Northport, New York, with her family. Besides writing, she loves music, theater, animals, and, of course, children of all ages.

ABOUT THE ILLUSTRATOR

Joy Allen has loved drawing all her life. She attended Choinards Art Institute in Los Angeles, California, for a year before getting married and starting a family. Allen is the mother of four grown children and has two grandchildren, who appear in some of her books. In four years, she illustrated thirty-two books, including picture books and early readers. She lives in California.